123836 EN
Frogfish, The

Rake, Jody Sullivan
ATOS BL 1.6
Points: 0.5

LG

Patterson Elementary School
3731 Lawrence Drive
Naperville, IL 60564

# The
# Frogfish

by Jody Sullivan Rake

**Consulting Editor:** Gail Saunders-Smith, PhD

Consultants: J. Charles Delbeek and Norton Chan
Aquarium Biologists
Waikiki Aquarium
University of Hawaii, Honolulu

Capstone
press®

Mankato, Minnesota

Pebble Plus is published by Capstone Press,
151 Good Counsel Drive, P.O. Box 669, Mankato, Minnesota 56002.
www.capstonepress.com

1  2  3  4  5  6  13  12  11  10  09  08

*Library of Congress Cataloging-in-Publication Data*
Rake, Jody Sullivan.
    The frogfish / by Jody Rake.
    p. cm. — (Weird animals)
    Includes bibliographical references and index.
    Summary: "Simple text and photos describe the unique homes, bodies, behaviors
and adaptations of frogfish" — Provided by publisher.
    ISBN-13: 978-1-4296-1738-3 (hardcover)
    ISBN-10: 1-4296-1738-1 (hardcover)
    1. Antennariidae — Juvenile literature. I. Title. II. Series.
QL638.A577R35 2008
597'.62 — dc22                                              2008004212

**Editorial Credits**
Jenny Marks, editor; Ted Williams and Kyle Grenz, designers; Jo Miller, photo researcher

**Photo Credits**
Alamy/WaterFrame, 14–15
Bruce Coleman Inc./Reinhard Dirscherl, 9
Getty Images Inc./Minden Pictures/Chris Newbert, 1
iStockphoto/Vebjern Karlsen, 7
Nature Production/Shinji Kusano, 13
Peter Arnold/Kelvin Aitken, 17; PHONE PHONE - Auteurs Brandelet Didier, 20–21; Reinhard Dirscherl, 10–11
Photo Researchers, Inc/Georgette Douwma, 4–5
Tom Stack & Associates, Inc./Dave Fleetham, 19
Visuals Unlimited/Ken Lucas, cover

## Note to Parents and Teachers

The Weird Animals set supports national science standards related to the characteristics
and behavior of animals. This book describes and illustrates frogfish. The images support
early readers in understanding the text. The repetition of words and phrases helps early
readers learn new words. This book also introduces early readers to subject-specific
vocabulary words, which are defined in the Glossary section. Early readers may need
assistance to read some words and to use the Table of Contents, Glossary, Read More,
Internet Sites, and Index sections of the book.

# Table of Contents

# Lumpy, Bumpy Fish

Frogfish are short, round fish.

Their bumpy bodies

look like rocks, plants, or sponges.

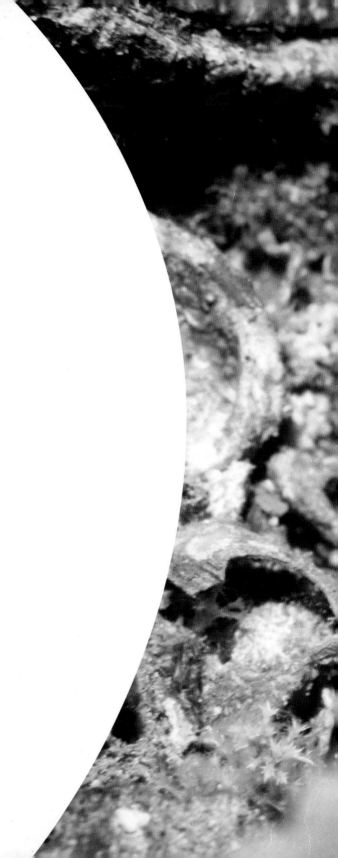

Frogfish can be many colors.

Their colors help them

blend into their surroundings.

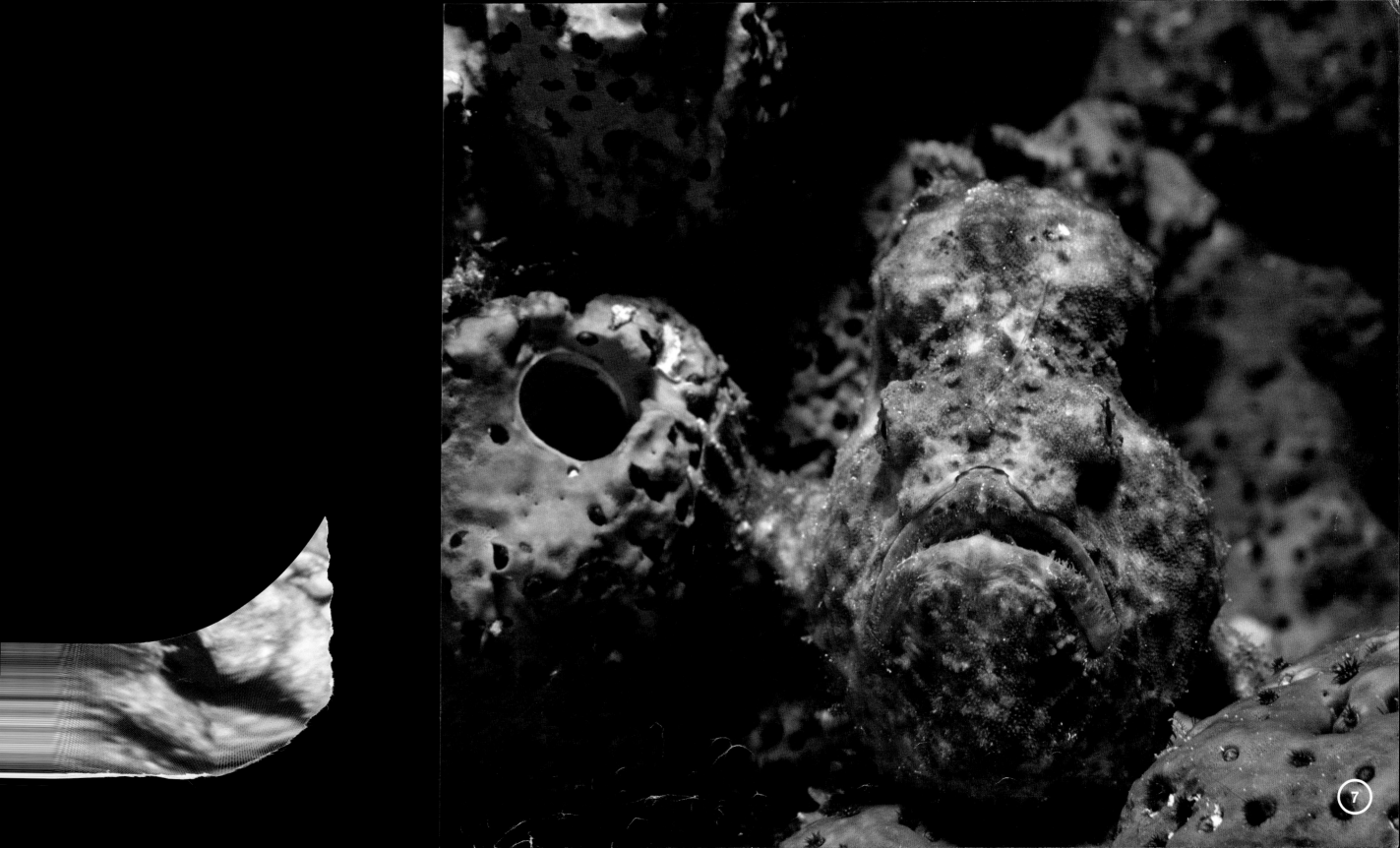

Frogfish are found
in tropical waters
all over the world.

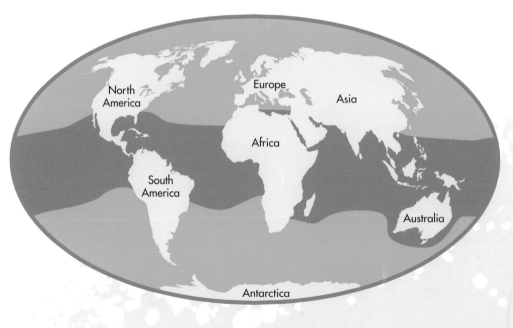

North
America

Europe

Asia

Africa

South
America

Australia

Antarctica

■ Frogfish Range

# Expert Fishers

Frogfish walk underwater.

They use their fins

like feet.

Frogfish find a spot to wait.

They wiggle

part of their dorsal fin.

It looks like something to eat.

Small curious fish swim near.

Snap!

The frogfish catches a fish

in a flash.

# The Life of a Frogfish

Most frogfish lay eggs in a clump.

The clump is called an egg raft.

The egg raft drifts in the open sea
until the eggs hatch.

When young frogfish hatch,

they are on their own.

Good luck, little frogfish!

Frogfish have

weird body parts.

But their bodies are perfect

for where they live.

# Glossary

blend — to look like a part of the surrounding area; frogfish blend into their underwater homes.

dorsal fin — the fins on the top of a fish

drift — to move with the waves in the ocean

egg raft — a group of eggs that stick together

hatch — to break out of an egg

pectoral fin — a fin on the side of a fish's body; frogfish walk on their pectoral fins.

sponge — an ocean animal with a soft body and no backbone

surroundings — the places and things you see around you

tropical — an area near the equator that is very warm

# Read More

**Coldiron, Deborah.** *Anglerfish*. Underwater World. Edina, Minn.: Abdo, 2008.

**Weber, Valerie J.** *Anglerfish*. Weird Wonders of the Deep. Milwaukee: Gareth Stevens, 2005.

# Internet Sites

FactHound offers a safe, fun way to find Internet sites related to this book. All of the sites on FactHound have been researched by our staff.

Here's how:

1. Visit *www.facthound.com*

2. Choose your grade level.

3. Type in this book ID **1429617381** for age-appropriate sites. You may also browse subjects by clicking on letters, or by clicking on pictures and words.

4. Click on the **Fetch It** button.

**FactHound will fetch the best sites for you!**

# Index

Word Count: 130

Grade: 1

Early-Intervention Level: 18